SCOTTIE PIPPEN
THE DO-EVERYTHING SUPERSTAR

BY BILL GUTMAN

MILLBROOK SPORTS WORLD
THE MILLBROOK PRESS
BROOKFIELD, CONNECTICUT

Library of Congress Cataloging-in-Publication Data
Gutman, Bill.
Scottie Pippen: the do-everything superstar / Bill Gutman.
p. cm.—(Millbrook sports world)
Includes bibliographical references and index.
Summary: Looks at the career of this basketball star who, in spite of
playing in the shadow of Michael Jordan, has become one of the
greatest all-around performers in the sport's history.
ISBN 0-7613-0223-9 (lib. bdg.)
1. Pippen, Scottie—Juvenile literature. 2. Basketball players—United
States—Biography—Juvenile literature. 3. Chicago Bulls (Basketball
team)—Juvenile literature. [1. Pippen, Scottie. 2. Basketball players.
3. Afro-Americans—Biography.] I. Title. II. Series.
GV884.P55G88   1997
796.323'092—dc21
[B]   97-1090   CIP   AC

Photographs courtesy of NBA Photos: cover (Barry Gossage); cover
inset (Nathaniel S. Butler), pp. 26 (Bill Baptist), 41 (Nathaniel S.
Butler), 42 (Scott Cunningham); Focus on Sports: pp. 3, 28, 32, 44, 46;
AP/Wide World Photos: pp. 4, 12, 18, 20, 23, 30, 31, 34, 35, 36, 38,
40; Claire Chapman: p. 8; Reuters/Corbis-Bettmann: p. 15.

Published by The Millbrook Press, Inc.
2 Old New Milford Road
Brookfield, Connecticut 06804

SCOTTIE PIPPEN

Of all the teams in the National Basketball Association, none played the Chicago Bulls tougher than the New York Knicks. So when the two teams met in the Eastern Conference Finals after the 1992–1993 season, many thought that the Knicks had a good chance to win.

It didn't matter that the Bulls were two-time defending NBA champions. Or that Chicago had the man considered to be the greatest basketball player of all time—Michael Jordan. Somehow, the Knicks' defensive-oriented game and rugged style of play often gave the Chicagoans fits.

Led by their star center, Patrick Ewing, the New Yorkers won the first two games of the series at their home arena, Madison Square Garden. Back in Chicago Stadium, the Bulls won the next two games to even the series. Then the

Scottie rose to the occasion during the Eastern Conference Finals against the New York Knicks in 1992–1993. Here, Scottie skies above the Knicks defenders en route to a 28-point performance in game three.

Bulls took game five at the "Garden" to grab a 3–2 lead. On Friday night, June 4, 1993, the two teams squared off again in Chicago for game six. This game was crucial to the Bulls. If the Bulls lost, they would have to return to New York for the seventh and deciding game.

Chicago fans were worried. Jordan wasn't shooting well in the series, hitting about 40 percent from the field instead of his usual 52 percent. More and more, the team was looking for its number two star, Scottie Pippen, to come up big. A 6-foot-7 (200-centimeter) forward, he was a lot like his teammate Jordan in many ways. He could do everything on the basketball court. And in game six he proved it all over again.

Chicago was in the lead for most of the game, but couldn't seem to break it open. Late in the final period, the Knicks began chipping away at the Bulls' seven-point lead. They were in a position to steal the game and tie the series. But two crucial shots saved the day. And both came from the hands of Scottie Pippen.

With the shot clock running down, Scottie got the ball deep in the right corner and let it fly. Swish! A three-pointer to keep the Bulls on top. A short time later the Bulls were looking to get the ball in close, and once again the New York defense closed them off. Again the shot clock ticked perilously close to zero. The ball was passed out to Scottie, who was well outside the top of the key. Again he let go for a long three-pointer. Again it hit nothing but net.

When the game ended, the Bulls had a 96–88 victory and had earned their way to a third-straight trip to the NBA Finals and another championship. Scottie Pippen came away with a 24-point, 6-rebound, 7-assist night that helped put his team on top.

"It's no secret," Bulls Coach Phil Jackson said afterward. "So goes Scottie Pippen, so goes Chicago."

Yet Scottie has played nearly his entire career in the huge shadow of Michael Jordan. Jordan was born with a natural talent and has worked hard to maintain his superior level of play. Although Scottie Pippen was not born with the same degree of natural ability, he, too, worked hard on his game and is now considered by many to be the second-best all-around player in the National Basketball Association.

Second best or not, Scottie found the road to the top quite difficult. In fact, he started his basketball career in a rather unusual way—by handing out towels and uniforms.

A SMALL TOWN LIFE

When you're born and grow up in a town of less than 4,000 people, no one expects you to become a superstar athlete someday, or to bask in the bright lights of a big city. It certainly wasn't expected of Scottie Pippen. He'd have a hard enough time struggling to find his place within his large family.

Scottie was born in Hamburg, Arkansas, on September 25, 1965. He was the youngest of 12 children born to Ethel and Preston Pippen. Mrs. Pippen stayed at home to raise her large family, while Mr. Pippen worked long hours at a local paper and plywood mill. The family was always very close.

Hamburg is a tiny town in southern Arkansas near the Louisiana border. At the time Scottie was born it had just 3,394 residents, as well as two shirt factories, a lumber company, and the paper mill.

There wasn't much to do in Hamburg, and perhaps that's why large families like Scottie's were so close. The Pippens were always together. And though Scottie was the baby of the family, he wasn't treated that way by his brothers and sisters.

"My sisters would always have me do little things for them," Scottie recalled. "They would have me doing this and doing that, but always for a couple of dollars. I did it because I was one of those kids who always wanted to have a couple of dollars in my pocket."

One thing the kids always did was play sports. Scottie, who was a small and very thin youngster, played baseball and basketball, but never seemed to excel in either sport. By the time he reached his teens, playing sports occupied a good deal of his time.

Scottie returns often to his tiny hometown of Hamburg, Arkansas, to which he has donated money to improve parks and sports facilities for kids. Here, visiting the home of a former high school teacher, Scottie takes time to read about his favorite subject—basketball.

"We used to play at the Pine Street courts," said Ron Martin, one of Scottie's boyhood friends. "It was when we were about 13 or 14. We played as late as we could, until this old man would run us off for making noise. When we played baseball, Scottie was on the Giants, I was on the A's.

"In basketball, we also must have played a million games of one-on-one. I was a little bit bigger than him, heavier, stronger, so I used to lean on him. Then, somewhere, he got big on me."

But Scottie didn't get big overnight. He was still small and thin as a teenager. In fact, his mother does not remember him as much of an athlete.

"He was just a nice boy," she said. "He was an average kid who didn't get into trouble. But he never made you think he'd do anything special."

Everyone liked Scottie. Dorothy Higginbotham, who was a guidance counselor at Hamburg High School and knew Scottie as he was growing up, said the same thing. "Scottie was well liked by his peers and his teachers," was the way she said it. "He didn't push himself on people."

Scottie played football in junior high school, but by the time he reached 10th grade at Hamburg High, he knew what he wanted to be—a player in the National Basketball Association. The only problem was he still wasn't very good. And soon after the school year began there was a family crisis that could have taken Scottie away from basketball forever.

SOME DIFFICULT CHOICES

One day when Scottie was in the 10th grade his father came home from a long shift at the paper mill. Shortly after, Mr. Pippen collapsed to the floor. He was rushed to the hospital where doctors told the family that he had suffered a massive stroke. After that, Mr. Pippen was partially paralyzed and had to stay in a wheelchair. He couldn't work, so everyone in the family would have to help out.

Scottie wanted to do his part. He talked about leaving school. But his mother and older brothers and sisters told him to stay. Most of them were already out of school and working. There was no reason for Scottie to quit.

He wasn't a very good basketball player then. In fact, he wasn't even 6 feet (183 centimeters) tall yet. He spent a year managing the football team, but came back to basketball for his senior year of 1982–1983. As a senior, Scottie was just 6 feet 1 (185 centimeters), and weighed only 145 pounds (66 kilograms). His high school coach, Donald Wayne, saw him as simply average.

"There was nothing special or flashy about him," the coach said. "People would ask all the time why I was starting him."

But Scottie was a consistent point guard who didn't make a lot of mistakes. And he had one important thing going for him: He loved the game and didn't want to give it up once his high school days were over. Yet not a single college called or came to scout him. It was apparent that there was no way he would get a scholarship or even be invited for a tryout.

Scottie didn't want his basketball days to end without a fight. He went to his coach and asked for help. Coach Wayne didn't want to discourage any student who wanted to go on to college. So he called his old college coach from Henderson State, Don Dyer. Dyer was now coaching at Central Arkansas University in Conway, north of Little Rock, the capital.

There was no way Coach Wayne could promise his friend that he was getting a star player. He simply told him that Scottie was an adequate point guard who would also make a good manager under a work-study program. Coach Wayne also mentioned that there were some big, older kids in the Pippen family and that Scottie might grow.

Dyer agreed to give Scottie a chance. The deal was that Scottie would attend Central Arkansas in the fall of 1983. He would be the basketball team manager and would qualify for an educational grant that would help pay his way through college. As for playing on the team, Scottie would have to show he was good enough to make it.

By the time he arrived at the Conway campus he had indeed grown. He was now 6 feet 3 (190 centimeters) and still very thin. But he played in as many pickup games with team members as he could, and Coach Dyer noticed that Scottie worked hard and held his own. He was very competitive alongside the varsity players. Then two players left the team shortly before the season began. Suddenly, Scottie found himself putting on a uniform instead of handing it out.

Scottie got into only 20 games for the Bears his freshman year. His playing time was limited. He averaged only 4.3 points a game and grabbed 59 rebounds. Playing against other small colleges with second-rate competition, Scottie seemed like a marginal player at best. But at least he was on the court.

BECOMING AN UNLIKELY STAR

Central Arkansas was an NAIA (National Association of Intercollegiate Athletics) school. Most of the topflight competition was at the larger, NCAA (National Collegiate Athletic Association) schools. The Bears played mainly state-wide opponents such as Ouachita Baptist and the University of the Ozarks. It wasn't much of a stage for an athlete to strut his stuff. Because of this, Central Arkansas had never sent a player to the NBA.

Scottie returned for his sophomore year in the fall of 1984. He had worked and practiced all summer. And he had grown. His teammates were surprised when he came back at a full 6 feet 5 (196 centimeters). Though he was still very thin at 165 pounds (75 kilograms), Scottie had long arms and huge hands. He was a much improved player, who could run and jump. In fact, he did almost everything well.

Scottie played in 19 games during his sophomore season and made huge progress. He averaged 18.5 points a game, hit 56.4 percent of his shots from the field, and grabbed 175 rebounds, an average of 9.2 a game. He was a different ballplayer from his freshman year, perhaps already the best on the team.

"I remember thinking at the end of his sophomore season that Scottie had a chance [at the NBA]," said Coach Dyer. "I'd seen Sidney Moncrief and Darrell Walker play at the University of Arkansas at the same stage, and they both made it. I thought Scottie was bigger and better."

At Central Arkansas, Scottie went from being team manager to team star. He worked extremely hard all four years, spending hours by himself just dribbling the basketball. As an NBA star, the hard work has paid off. He can dribble equally well with both hands—here he goes left to get around a defender.

The question was, would he ever get a real chance? Central Arkansas didn't put him on a national stage and wouldn't as long as he stayed there. But Scottie never considered transferring to a major school. Instead, he returned for his junior year and had grown again. Now he was 6 feet 6 (198 centimeters) and a solid 185 pounds (84 kilograms). There was no denying that he had grown into a fine player.

Scottie was now averaging nearly 20 points a game and becoming a better defender and rebounder. Assistant Coach Arch Jones marveled at the way Scottie kept his game together during this period of rapid physical growth.

"He was able to take the skills he had learned when he was smaller and use them when he was bigger," said Jones. "His arms are so long, his hands so big that he really plays like someone 6-foot-10 or 6-foot-11."

At the end of his junior year, Scottie was averaging 19.8 points and 9.2 rebounds, but there was still no interest shown in him from any NBA scouts or teams. Most of them didn't know he existed. As he prepared to return to Central Arkansas for his final season of 1986–1987, he knew it would be his last chance to show the NBA people he was for real.

STEPPING UP TO NUMBER ONE

Scottie returned to Central Arkansas at his full height of 6 feet 7 (200 centimeters) and proceeded to have his greatest year. He averaged 23.6 points and 10 rebounds a game. He also hit 59.2 percent of his shots from the field. It was obvious that he was ready for the next step.

But once again there would be no championship for the Bears. Playing in a postseason tournament would have given Scottie some kind of national exposure, but it didn't happen. In addition, Scottie was a low-key person who didn't speak much and never bragged about his achievements. But he still wanted to play in the NBA. If he didn't get a chance or didn't make it, however, he knew he would return home to Hamburg.

"I knew some guys back home in Arkansas and they would help me find some kind of job," he said. "I don't know what, exactly. But I knew they would come up with something for me."

What Scottie didn't know was that someone was already coming up with something for him. In February of Scottie's senior year NBA scouting agent Marty Blake had seen him play. Blake then called Jerry Krause, the general manager of the Chicago Bulls, and told him that Scottie might be worth looking at.

Krause got his first glimpse of Scottie at a postseason amateur tournament in Portsmouth, Virginia. He was impressed.

"The players came out for warm-ups, hadn't even shot the ball," the Bulls' GM said. "Here's this guy. He's got the longest arms I've ever seen. I've always been very big on long arms and big hands. I thought to myself, 'There's something special.' And when I looked around, everybody else was murmuring, too."

Krause was already thinking about Scottie as a possible second-round draft pick. But when Scottie showed up at a number of NBA pre-draft tryout camps, things changed. Arch Jones, the assistant coach at Central Arkansas, went with Scottie to one of them in Chicago.

"I never realized how good he really was until I saw him with all the other players at the tryout camp," Jones recalled. "Scottie made a move. He came in from the right and banked the ball off the backboard with his left hand. And when he'd go up the middle . . . dunk city."

Suddenly, Scottie Pippen was a secret no longer. He was a razor-thin youngster who never showed a change of expression. Yet he had incredible skills, instincts, and jumping ability. Many of his skills had been honed by hours of practice in Hamburg.

When Chicago Bulls General Manager Jerry Krause first saw Scottie, he said that Scottie had the longest arms he had ever seen. In the NBA, Scottie has always used his long arms and huge hands to great advantage in scoring over defenders.

"Nobody knows how hard I worked alone on dribbling and just feeling the ball in my hands," Scottie said.

By the time the tryout camps were over, almost every team in the NBA wanted to know more about him. Krause knew he still wanted him. But now he was worried that Scottie wouldn't last until the second round of the draft. The Bulls had the eighth pick in the first round. Krause was worried that even that would be too late.

So the cagey GM made a deal with the Seattle Supersonics. The Sonics picked fifth and took Scottie. Chicago then took center Olden Polynice with their first pick. The two teams then traded picks and Scottie became the property of the Chicago Bulls.

Just four years after going to Central Arkansas as the manager of the basketball team, Scottie Pippen was a first-round draft choice in the National Basketball Association. His longtime dream was about to become reality.

PLAYING ALONGSIDE A GUY NAMED MICHAEL

The team Scottie Pippen would join in 1987–1988 had had just one winning season since 1976–1977. But in 1984, the team had drafted a 6-foot-6 (198-centimeter) shooting guard out of the University of North Carolina. His name was Michael Jordan, and he had been college basketball's Player of the Year for two straight seasons.

Jordan took the NBA by storm. He was Rookie of the Year in 1984–1985, averaging 28.2 points a game. He was a spectacular player that fans everywhere wanted to see, even though the team finished at 38–44. The next year Michael missed most of the season with a broken foot. But in the 1986–1987 season, he was simply amazing.

That year, Michael won the scoring title with an average of 37.1 points per game. With a 40–42 record, however, Chicago needed more talent to go with their spectacular superstar. Along with Scottie, the club drafted a 6-foot-10 (208-centimeter) power forward named Horace Grant, who was the 10th pick of the first round. The Bulls hoped that Pippen and Grant would give them two new impact players.

"If Scottie didn't become the player I thought he could be," General Manager Krause said, "he'd have gone down as Krause's folly. I'd have been ripped from pillar to post."

When Scottie joined the team for the start of practice, both Krause and Coach Doug Collins were immediately impressed. Scottie wanted to take on the best. He insisted on guarding Jordan in team practices over and over again. "I figured he couldn't do anything to me that he hadn't already done to somebody else," Scottie said. It was apparent that the rookie was ready to learn.

Scottie was a role player in his rookie season. He was in 79 games, playing about 21 minutes in each. (An NBA game is 48 minutes long.) He averaged 7.9 points a game, grabbed 298 rebounds, had 91 steals, and 52 blocked shots. The other first-round choice, Horace Grant, averaged 7.7 points a game and grabbed 447 rebounds.

Both rookies added a new dimension to the team. But the jury was still out on how good they would be in the long run. Besides Jordan, the only other Bulls player considered a star was power forward Charles Oakley. But with the young players contributing, the team looked to be turning things around. In fact, they put together their best season in years.

The Bulls finished in a tie for second place with Atlanta in the Central Division. Each had a 50–32 record, four games behind the first-place Detroit Pistons. Jordan won another scoring title with a 35-point average, while Oakley gathered in 1,066 rebounds.

As a rookie, Scottie practiced hard against Bulls superstar Michael Jordan. He knew that Michael could teach him more than anyone. Here, Scottie (right) high-fives Jordan while Horace Grant (left, with glasses) watches. Grant was drafted the same year as Scottie, and the two joined with Jordan to become the heart of the Bulls' first three title teams.

In the first round of the playoffs, the Bulls topped the Cleveland Cavaliers, 3 games to 2. Then they were beaten by Detroit in the Conference semifinals, 4–1. Scottie averaged 10 points in 10 playoff games.

Scottie probably remembered many things from his rookie year. He had fulfilled his longtime dream of playing in the NBA. He was a member of an improving team led by the great Michael Jordan. But perhaps more than anything else, he remembered his mother telling him about the first time his father saw him play.

As a result of his stroke, Preston Pippen couldn't travel to Chicago. So Scottie sent home a videotape of his very first pro game. His mother called to tell him his father's reaction.

"The stroke took away my father's ability to speak," Scottie said. "But my mom told me that when he watched the tape he cried."

During the offseason, Scottie needed surgery to correct a problem in his back. He missed the entire 1988 preseason and the first eight games of the regular campaign. But then he returned full strength. He had already learned a lot just from watching teammate Michael Jordan, who not only was the most spectacular offensive player in the game but also one of the best all-around.

Jordan could do everything on the basketball court. He was a dynamic scorer, he could bring the ball up the floor, and was an outstanding passer. In spite of working so hard on offense, he also played tough, nonstop defense. And he could go up and get the ball under the boards. Scottie Pippen was working on all these phases of his game, as well.

It wasn't long after Scottie returned to the team that he became a starter at the small-forward position. The team had made one major change. Charles Oakley was traded to the New York Knicks for 7-foot-1 (216-centimeter) center Bill Cartwright. Horace Grant moved to Oakley's power-forward spot. Cartwright, a good scorer and tough defender, was in the middle. Sam Vincent and John Paxson shared the other guard spots opposite Jordan.

The 1988–1989 season was one of adjustment with a new center and two young players starting at forward. The club finished at 47–35, three games under their record of a year earlier. But they were in the playoffs again, and both Pippen and Grant had shown tremendous improvement.

Jordan won another scoring title with a 32.5 average, but now Scottie was the number two scorer. In 73 games, he averaged 14.4 points with a high game of 31. He had 445 rebounds and was second to Jordan with 139 steals. Grant averaged 12 points a game and led the team with 681 rebounds.

In the playoffs, the Bulls whipped the Cleveland Cavaliers in five games, then topped the Knicks in six to reach the Conference Finals against the Detroit Pistons. Chicago played the eventual NBA champs tough, losing in six hard-fought games. In the sixth and final game, something happened that would come back to haunt Scottie for several years.

The game was just a few minutes old when Scottie took a hard elbow to the head from the Pistons' center Bill Laimbeer. He was knocked unconscious for a brief time, then helped to the sidelines, where he stayed for the rest of the game. Later, Scottie was criticized for not being a gamer, for not having the guts to return in the biggest game of the year.

But Scottie had tried to return. "I wanted to go back in," he said. "I asked and asked to go back. The doctor and Jerry Krause wouldn't let me. I wanted to say, 'Can we stop everything? Can we play that game over again? Right now?'"

The season ended on a sour note for both Scottie and the team. And there would be another roadblock the following year when Scottie's character would be questioned once again.

During his rookie season, Scottie learned all about the rough play in the NBA. Here, he tries to keep the ball away from the Cavaliers' Brad Daugherty (right) and Hot Rod Williams (left) as teammate Dave Corzine looks on.

CHAMPIONS AT LAST

The 1989–1990 season was another step in the right direction for Scottie and the Bulls. Though the team seemed to be improving steadily, management decided to make a change. Phil Jackson, a former NBA player with the Knicks, became the new head coach. Jackson was a different kind of coach. He was an avid reader who loved philosophy. It helped him to mold and motivate his team. And he knew the X's and O's of basketball, as well.

Under Jackson, the ballclub finished the regular season with a 55–27 record, four games behind the defending champion Pistons in the Central Division. Jordan was amazing as usual, leading the league in scoring and steals. Many were beginning to call him the best player of all time.

As for Scottie, he had really come into his own that season, his third in the NBA. He was second on the team in scoring with 16.5 points a game. He was also second to Jordan in steals with 211 and third in the entire league. He grabbed 547 rebounds, just 18 fewer than Michael, and he led the Bulls with 101 blocked shots.

In other words, he was becoming the same kind of great all-around player that Jordan was. It was a memorable year. He was selected to play in the NBA All-Star Game for the first time and had a brand-new home built for his parents in Hamburg. Then it was time for the playoffs, and many experts predicted that the Bulls would unseat the defending champion Pistons.

The two teams would eventually meet in the Eastern Conference Finals for the right to play for the championship. But the playoffs didn't turn out to be a happy time for Scottie. In the Conference semifinals, the Bulls were meeting

By 1990, Scottie had become a fine, all-around player. Here, he uses his long arms to defend against a drive by the Bullets' Ledell Eackles. He finished third in the league that year in steals.

the Philadelphia 76ers. Midway through the series Scottie learned that his father had died. The Bulls won the series in five games and got set to meet the Pistons, but Scottie Pippen was now playing with a heavy heart.

He still gave it his best. The Bulls and the Pistons battled evenly for six games. Now it was down to a seventh and final game to see which ballclub would go on to the Finals. Scottie started the game, but didn't seem right. He was missing shots and looking out of sync with his teammates. After hitting just one of 10 shots, he came out.

Fans saw him sitting on the bench with an icepack on his head. He never returned to the game and the Bulls lost, 93–74. Scottie had scored just two points. Later, it was revealed that he had come down with a very painful migraine headache. Once again people said it was an excuse, claiming that he lacked guts and couldn't stay in a big game. It was an unfortunate end to a fine season.

"I'd never had a migraine before," Scottie said later. "Migraine headaches happen to people all the time. It just happened to me at the wrong time. People want results, not excuses. If I had been able to play up to my ability, I think we would have won. I know that when I'm at full strength, I am one of the best players in the game."

What Scottie didn't say until a year later was that he had been so frightened by the migraine that he went to the hospital a few days later and had a brain scan because the pain was still there.

"It was like someone had put an ice pick in my head," he said. "I was afraid I was dying."

Doctors prescribed the eyeglasses he now wears off the court to prevent the migraines from recurring. He also sought out the advice of former NBA stars like Julius Erving and Kareem Abdul-Jabbar. One of the greatest players ever, Abdul-Jabbar also had recurring migraines throughout his career.

When Scottie returned for the 1990–1991 season he had made some changes in his lifestyle: "Now I eat a good breakfast, then don't eat again until after the game," he said. "I make sure I get my sleep. I always take a nap in the afternoon on the day of a game. I lie in bed, visualize the game, think about who I am guarding and the things he likes to do. It all helps."

Even with his two-point final game, Scottie averaged 19.3 points in 15 play-off games in 1990. He had managed to elevate his game in the postseason. Now both he and his teammates were ready to make a serious run at the NBA title. Scottie knew it was time for him to rise to the top.

Early in the 1990–1991 season, the Bulls were struggling a bit. Scottie wasn't shooting well. Coach Jackson told him to relax and not worry about his shooting. He told him to concentrate on his all-around game. That night, against the Los Angeles Clippers, Scottie went out and posted a triple-double (double figures in three statistical categories), with 13 points, 13 rebounds, and 12 assists. The team won.

"That really showed everyone, including Scottie, just what he could do," the coach said. "We went on to win seven in a row, and that sent us into the rest of the season."

As for Scottie, he knew he was prospering under Coach Jackson, as well.

"I think when Phil took over everyone found it easier to accept their roles because they had the freedom to try contributing a little more," Scottie said.

Coach Jackson seemed to get real pleasure at watching Scottie's game develop and expand. "[Scottie's] role here has grown and grown," the coach said. "As a player starting out, you could see his possibilities. He could rebound, yet still dribble the length of the court. He could post up. He had these slashing sorts of moves. You knew he could become a very good player, but you didn't know how good."

The Bulls won the Central Division title with a 61–21 record as Scottie had his greatest season yet. He averaged 17.8 points in 82 games, was second on the team to Grant in rebounds with 595, led the team with 511 assists and 93 blocks and was fifth in the league with 193 steals. And he was named to the NBA second team All-Defensive Team.

The Bulls whipped through the playoffs. They topped the New York Knicks in three straight, then beat the 76ers 4–1, and in the Conference Finals toppled the defending two-time champion Pistons in four straight games. Now they had to meet the Los Angeles Lakers, led by the great Earvin "Magic" Johnson, for the NBA championship.

After the Lakers won the opening game, Chicago took charge and won the next four. They were champions, at last. In the final game, both Pippen and Jordan were all over the court. Each played the entire 48 minutes and had 10 steals between them. And Scottie led all scorers with 32 points in a 108–101 title-clinching victory.

Scottie averaged 21.6 points in 17 playoff games, had 151 rebounds, 99 assists, and 42 steals. He had played a major role in the Bulls' first-ever championship. Around the league, rival players now knew the kind of player Scottie had become. Perhaps Bernard King of the Washington Bullets said it best.

"Scottie is a transformed player," King explained, "one of the few guys who's a complete player in the NBA."

As the Bulls drove toward their first championship in 1991, Scottie had become an All-Star. His scoring average was up to 17.8 and he was tough to stop, especially for smaller men like Houston's Sam Cassell.

A SUPERSTAR IN HIS OWN RIGHT

During the next two seasons, the Bulls proved that they were a great team, and Scottie Pippen proved that he was a great player. Chicago won another pair of championships, making it three in a row. They defeated the Portland Trail Blazers in the finals in 1992, and the Phoenix Suns in 1993, both in six games. And Scottie's numbers were up across the board.

He averaged 21 points in 1992, and 18.6 points in 1993, and made the All-NBA second team and third team in those years. He was also a first-teamer on the All-Defensive Team. His abilities were no longer a secret.

Scottie proudly holds the NBA championship trophy after the Bulls defeated the Portland Trail Blazers in 1992 for their second-straight title. Joining him are Michael Jordan (right) and Horace Grant.

"As more teams pressed us," Coach Jackson said, "we decided we had to become more creative in our response. . . . We came up with the thought of Scottie as a third ball advancer, of an offense that attacked at multiple points. From that position, he started being able to take control, to make decisions. And he became a bit of everything."

Bill Walton, a former star NBA center, was one who felt Scottie had just about reached the top.

"You think about it and Scottie Pippen might just be the second-best all-around player in the league," Walton said. "Who's better, outside of Michael? Who does more things?"

Scottie himself was more at ease now. He had finally lived down the incidents in 1989 and 1990 that brought him so much criticism. He had proven that he could perform in a big game.

"I definitely put all that to rest," Scottie has said. "I needed a championship. I needed a chance to prove that I was a money ballplayer. Three championship rings don't hurt when it comes to burying the 'soft' business."

The other thing Scottie had to live with—as did all the Bulls—was playing in the shadow of Michael Jordan. In the 1992–1993 season, Jordan had won his seventh straight scoring title. He was a three-time NBA Most Valuable Player and had been the MVP in the Finals of all three Chicago titles. Now nearly everyone, past and present, was calling him the best basketball player of all time.

Scottie never fooled himself into thinking he was another Michael Jordan.

"Sure, I wanted more [recognition and shots] early in my career," Scottie has said. "It was also hard always being compared to Michael. I heard things that players on other teams with superstars didn't hear. Things like, 'Well, Michael held up his end as usual, but Scottie didn't do enough.' I just came to realize that

Scottie uses his speed and moves to drive to the hoop against Charles Barkley (left) and the Phoenix Suns during the 1993 NBA Finals. The Bulls prevailed to win a third-straight championship.

it was a unique situation with Michael because of how truly great he is. I've come to terms with my role on this team, to do the things I can do. I'll never be the scorer Michael is. I couldn't put up those numbers even if I tried."

But Scottie was truly enjoying being himself. In the summer of 1992 he was a member of the first U.S. Olympic "Dream Team." The team included the first NBA players allowed to participate in the Olympics. With Jordan, Magic Johnson, Larry Bird, and other greats, Scottie helped the club to easily win the gold medal.

After the Bulls' third-straight title in 1992-1993, some experts felt that the team had the talent to win three more in a row. But in the off-season, something happened that changed the lives of everyone on the team.

In July 1993, Michael Jordan's father, James, was reported missing while on a business trip. Several weeks later, Mr. Jordan's car was located in North Carolina, and shortly afterward his body was found in a nearby creek. James Jordan had been shot to death in a random robbery. Two 18-year-olds were charged with the crime.

Michael Jordan went into mourning. His father had attended every Bulls game and was also Michael's best friend. In October, Michael shocked the sports world by announcing he was retiring from basketball. He said he had nothing left to prove and decided to pursue another dream—to become a big-league baseball player. The Chicago White Sox signed him and sent him to the minor leagues.

Suddenly, the Bulls were without their leader and superstar. Like everyone else, Scottie was surprised by Jordan's sudden retirement.

"I guess this summer was hard on him," Scottie said, referring to the death of Michael's father. "I'm sure that Michael knows that physically he can still play the game. But the question is: Does he have any desire to play it?"

The U.S. "Dream Team" won the basketball gold medal at the 1992 Olympic Games. Here, Michael Jordan raises his arm in victory, while teammates Clyde Drexler (right) and Scottie enjoy the moment.

With Jordan gone, the pressure of winning a fourth title suddenly fell on Scottie. He was expected to be the new team leader. The first time Coach Jackson saw Scottie after Jordan's announcement, he said, "The saddle goes on your back. We're going to ride you."

But Scottie knew he couldn't be Michael. "If you look at what I've done statistically over the last few years," he said, "nothing has dramatically changed. I'm not trying to be Michael. I don't need to be for this team to win."

There was one important addition to the Bulls in 1993–1994. During the off-season, the team signed 6-foot-11 (210-centimeter) Toni Kukoc from Croatia (part of the former Yugoslavia) in Europe. Kukoc was considered one of the best players in Europe and a player who could become an NBA star. The team gave Kukoc a six-year contract worth $25 million.

This didn't make Scottie happy. He was also on a multiyear contract, but earning about $2.5 million per year, less than Kukoc. With Jordan gone, Scottie felt he should be the highest-paid member of the team.

When Michael Jordan left the Bulls in 1993 to try his hand at baseball, Scottie paid a visit to his friend during spring training. Here, Scottie dons a Chicago White Sox jacket and takes his turn on the pitching mound.

There was even talk of trading Scottie to another club. But fortunately for the Bulls, that didn't happen.

Saddled by an ankle injury, Scottie missed a handful of games at the outset of the season. When he was back at full strength, the team was struggling at 5–7. Many were already saying they couldn't win without Michael.

Then on November 30, 1993, the Bulls met the tough Phoenix Suns. Scottie came out and took over. Playing his usual, all-around game, he scored 29 points, and added 11 rebounds and 6 assists. The Bulls won, 132–113. And with Scottie leading the way, the team won 15 of its next 18 games and once again were up among the best teams in the league.

When the season ended, the Bulls had a 55–27 record. They finished two games behind Atlanta in the Central Division. Many felt that the Bulls were still the best team in the league and had a good chance to win a fourth-straight title. And Scottie Pippen had taken over and put together his greatest season yet.

In 72 games, he averaged 22 points, eighth best in the league. He was second on the Bulls (after Horace Grant) with 629 rebounds, led the team with 403 assists, and was second in the league with 2.93 steals a game. This time he was named to the All-NBA first team and was a first teamer on the All-Defensive Team. He also started in his third-straight midseason All-Star Game and was named the Most Valuable Player. Scottie had truly arrived as a superstar in his own right.

Then came the playoffs. Once again the Bulls met their bitter rivals, the New York Knicks, in the Eastern Conference semifinals. When the Knicks won the first two games at Madison Square Garden in New York, Scottie knew it was time for his team to step up.

"I don't think our problem is offense," he noted. "I think it's stopping them on defense and not letting them get second shots. We have to win the third game."

A proud Scottie holds the Most Valuable Player trophy after scoring 29 points in the 1994 NBA All-Star Game, which was won by the East, 127–118.

Back in Chicago, the Bulls blew a 22-point lead and needed a basket in the final 1.8 seconds to overcome a one-point Knicks lead. Coach Jackson set up a play in which Scottie would be a decoy and Toni Kukoc would take the last shot. But when the team returned to the court, Scottie stayed on the bench. Kukoc hit a long, three-pointer to give the Bulls an exhilarating 104–102 victory.

It was revealed later that Scottie had refused to go back in. Maybe it was his pride. He had wanted that last shot—all great players want the ball. But sitting out despite a coach's decision was a mistake, and he knew it. Later, he apologized.

"I put it behind me," he said. "I apologized to the team and to Phil Jackson. You always learn from mistakes. I just keep moving and try to do better."

The series finally came down to a seventh game at Madison Square Garden. The Knicks wound up winning, 87–77, despite Scottie scoring 20 points and grabbing 16 rebounds. And had it not been for a controversial foul call on Scottie in game five, there might not have even been a seventh game. Many felt the Bulls were playing as well as any team in the league when their season ended.

Scottie meets the press after refusing to reenter a playoff game against the Knicks when teammate Toni Kukoc was selected by Coach Jackson to take the last shot. He later apologized to his teammates, promising to learn from the experience and move on.

A CELEBRITY SUPERSTAR

As an NBA superstar, Scottie found new ways to use his celebrity status. In 1993 the Morley Candy Makers of Chicago produced a candy bar named after him. But the purpose of the candy bar was not to make money for Scottie. The candy bar was being sold to area schools and fundraising organizations. They could buy the bars at a high discount and keep the profit from reselling them.

He also formed the Scottie Pippen Youth Foundation to help youngsters in the Chicago area, and in September of 1994, Scottie organized a charity basket-

Scottie has always kept busy off the court. He has his own youth foundation and has done a great deal of charity work on behalf of youngsters. He also helped promote a new line of basketball cards.

ball game to be played in the Bulls' longtime arena, Chicago Stadium, which was about to be torn down. The team would start the 1994–1995 season at the brand-new United Center.

The Scottie Pippen Ameritech All Star Classic featured a number of NBA stars, including Michael Jordan, who at the time of that event was still playing minor-league baseball. The game raised some $175,000 for Scottie's Youth Foundation and for PUSH/Excel. Founded by the Reverend Jesse Jackson, PUSH/

Excel works to improve education standards and help youngsters achieve academic excellence.

After the game, the Reverend Jackson praised athletes like Scottie who commit to helping America's youth.

"High-profile athletes are impact educators who help to set the moral and social climate for society generally, but for our young people in particular," Jackson said.

Scottie also felt that the game served an important purpose.

"The game is a lot of fun, but most importantly it allows me and my fellow pros to give a little back to the city where I will always have my fondest memories. I'm glad we can be on the same team to provide a better future for the youth of Chicago."

On the court in 1994–1995, Scottie had another stellar season. He was an All-Star at midseason, was first team All-NBA and first team All-Defensive Team. He averaged 21.4 points a game, had a career high 639 rebounds, and led the league in steals with 232. He also led the club in assists, as well as in the other categories. But that wasn't the big news that year.

The Bulls had taken a hit early in the season when Horace Grant left the team due to free agency, signing with the Orlando Magic. But in the final month of the season, Michael Jordan returned. Jordan had decided he wasn't going to make it as a major-league baseball player and also realized how much he missed basketball. Still a bit rusty, Jordan nevertheless showed flashes of his old brilliance. Chicago finished the regular season at 47–35. The team made it to the Eastern Conference semifinals before losing to the Shaquille O'Neal-led Orlando Magic in six games.

Everyone looked to 1995–1996. Jordan had once again dedicated himself to basketball. And in the off-season, the team signed forward Dennis Rodman. Rodman was a showman who thrived on the publicity he got from his outrageous

behavior and looks. His hair was a different color almost every night, and his body was covered with tattoos.

But on the court, Rodman was a ferocious competitor and the best rebounder in the league. If he got along with Jordan and Pippen, the Bulls would have the best trio of superstars in the NBA.

COMPLETE RECOGNITION AND ANOTHER TITLE

It was apparent as soon as the Bulls came out of the gate in 1995 that Coach Phil Jackson had molded a super team. Veteran guard Ron Harper teamed with Jordan in the backcourt. Scottie and Rodman were at forward. And 7-foot-2 (218-centimeter) Luc Longley was the starting center. This team could score. But it was their great defense that brought them victory after victory.

When the Bulls came into Madison Square Garden in late January to play the Knicks, they had an unbelievable 34–3 record. They were on pace to be the first NBA team to reach 70 victories in a season. Jordan was back in his old form, once again leading the league in scoring, and Rodman was the top rebounder. But in the minds of many, it was the all-around game of Scottie Pippen that really made this latest version of the Bulls go.

"He's the best player in the league, by far," the Los Angeles Lakers' Cedric Ceballos said of Scottie. "Nobody's even close to him. He captures every essence of what a basketball player should be."

In 1994–1995, Scottie's game was better than ever. He was a first team All-NBA choice and a first teamer on the All-Defensive team. Here, his speed enables him to complete a fast break against the Knicks with a big slam dunk.

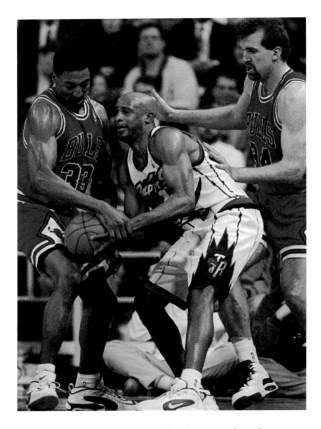

Scottie's all-around talent makes him a force to be reckoned with on the court. Here, he strips the ball from Toronto Raptors guard Alvin Robertson with Bulls teammate Bill Wennington backing him up.

The Indiana Pacers' guard Mark Jackson echoed this thought. "He's just incredible, a joy to watch," explained Jackson. "Jordan may be the best of all time, but today, Scottie Pippen is the best player in the game."

Scottie had become the prototype all-around player. At 6 feet 7, he was considered mid-sized, yet he could check anyone defensively, from hulking power forwards to slick shooting guards.

"I don't think any player has an effect on whether you win or lose on both ends of the court like he does," said Indiana coach Larry Brown. "Anybody who appreciates the game and loves it would feel the same way I do."

As for Scottie, he seemed to have even more confidence on the court. Even with Michael Jordan back, he felt secure in his position within the team and within the league.

"I think people were able to see what I could do as a player when Michael was away from the game," he said. "I'm the leader of the team. I'm the one who more or less runs the offense. I just have a lot of confidence now. I'm at ease with my game."

It was also apparent that the two superstars had deep respect for one another. Asked if he would have returned to the Bulls if Scottie had been traded to another team, Michael answered, "No, definitely no. That says how much I respect Scottie."

Scottie also made his feelings clear. "Michael will always be Michael," he said, "the greatest that ever played. But it is amazing that we're still together. In fact, it's an honor that we're still together. We are two of the top talents in the league. It's been an honor to have played with him for most of my career."

It was a record-setting year for the Bulls. The team finished the regular season with a 72–10 record, the best in NBA history. Jordan won his eighth scoring title

When rebounding ace Dennis Rodman joined the Bulls in 1995–1996, the team became nearly unbeatable. Scottie, too, can rebound with the best of them as he goes skyward to grab a ball against the Knicks.

with a 30.4 average. Scottie averaged 19.4 points and put up his usual great across-the-board numbers. That was expected of him now.

The Bulls were heavy favorites to win the playoffs. They opened by sweeping the Miami Heat in three-straight games. Then they topped the Knicks, 4–1. And in the Conference Finals, they surprised everyone by sweeping powerful

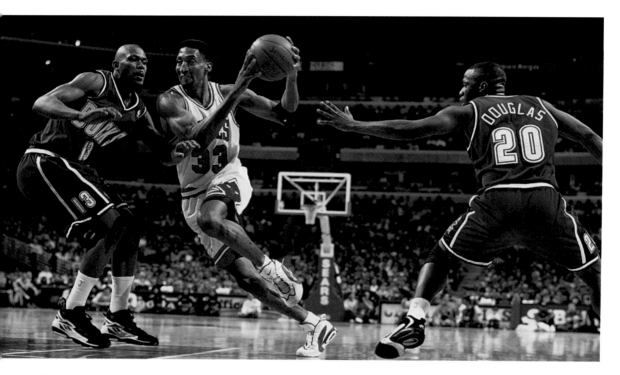

Scottie Pippen in full stride is a nearly unstoppable player. Milwaukee Bucks Glenn Robinson (left) and Sherman Douglas look almost frozen as Scottie jets to the basket.

Orlando in four-straight games. Now they were in the finals against the Seattle SuperSonics, a team that had won 64 games during the regular season.

Many believed that the Sonics, led by guard Gary Payton and forward Shawn Kemp, might give the Bulls a tussle. But Chicago won the first three games to all but wrap it up. Seattle battled back to take the next two. But then in game six at the United Center, the Bulls roared to a fourth NBA crown, winning 87–75.

People began talking dynasty when the Bulls did it again in 1996–1997. They finished at 69–13 and roared into the playoffs favored to win their fifth title in seven years. Again Michael Jordan was the star, with Scottie right beside him.

It was a typical great all-around year for Scottie. Not surprisingly, he was named to the All-Defensive Team and put up outstanding numbers. Without counting the first two seasons when Scottie was adjusting to NBA play, his career numbers are close to 20 points, 8 rebounds, and 7 assists a game.

In the playoffs, the Bulls topped the Washington Bullets in three straight games. Then they whipped the Atlanta Hawks in five, 4–1, and in the Conference Finals topped the Miami Heat in five games. The Finals would match the Bulls against the very tough Utah Jazz. But led by Jordan and Pippen, Chicago won it in six games to take their fifth championship of the decade.

The final game was a 90–86 victory at the United Center, and the fans went wild. When Jordan was named the Most Valuable Player in the Finals, he immediately went over to Scottie and told his teammate to hold the trophy aloft with him. Later, Jordan said that Scottie was also deserving of the award.

"I'll keep the trophy, but I'll give Scottie the car [the other part of the MVP prize]," Michael quipped.

Scottie had 23 points in the final game, once again reminding everyone just how good he was. In fact, he is now one of the most recognizable athletes in the world. During the summer of 1996 he was a member of the second U.S. Olympic "Dream Team," adding another gold medal to his trophy case.

He lives in a beautiful home near Chicago, yet returns often to his hometown of Hamburg, Arkansas. He has donated money to improve parks and sports facilities for the kids there.

There is no doubt that Scottie Pippen is one of the NBA's great success stories. And now he's a confident superstar. Asked recently—for probably the millionth time—if he wanted to be like Mike, Scottie answered graciously.

"No. I want to be like Scottie. That's all I can be and all I ever want to be."

SCOTTIE PIPPEN: HIGHLIGHTS

1965   Born on September 25 in Hamburg, Arkansas.

1987   Averages 23.6 points and 10 rebounds as a senior at Central Arkansas
        University.
        Picked by Seattle SuperSonics on first round of the NBA draft. Immediately
        traded to Chicago Bulls.

1990   Selected to play in NBA All-Star Game.
        Finishes third in NBA in steals with 211.

1991   Named to NBA All-Defensive Second Team.
        Helps Bulls to their first NBA championship.

1992   Averages 21 points a game.
        Voted starter in NBA All-Star Game.
        Named to All-NBA Second Team.
        Named to NBA All-Defensive First Team.
        Helps Bulls win their second-straight NBA championship.
        Member of the gold medal-winning U.S. Olympic basketball "Dream Team."

1993   Helps Bulls win their third-straight NBA championship.

1994   Named Most Valuable Player in NBA All-Star Game.
        Averages career best 22 points per game.
        Finishes second in NBA in steals with 211.
        Named to All-NBA First Team.

1995   Averages 21.4 points a game.
        Grabs career high 639 rebounds.
        Leads NBA in steals with 232.

1996   Member of the second gold medal-winning U.S. Olympic Dream Team.
        Helps Bulls to record-setting 72–10 season and their fourth NBA championship
        in six years.

1997   Voted starter in All-Star Game.
        Named to first team All-Defensive Team.
        Helps Bulls win fifth NBA championship in seven years.

FIND OUT MORE

Bjarkman, Peter C. *Sports Great Scottie Pippen*. Springfield, NJ: Enslow, 1996.

Gutman, Bill. *Michael Jordan: Basketball to Baseball and Back*. Brookfield, CT: Millbrook Press, 1995.

Gutman, Bill. *NBA High Flyers*. New York: Pocket Books, 1995.

McMane, Fred. *Scottie Pippen*. New York: Chelsea House, 1996.

Weber, Bruce. *Pro Basketball Megastars*. New York: Scholastic, 1996.

How to write to Scottie Pippen:
Scottie Pippen
c/o Chicago Bulls
One Magnificent Mile
980 N. Michigan Avenue, Suite 1600
Chicago, IL 60611

INDEX